Tenochtitlan

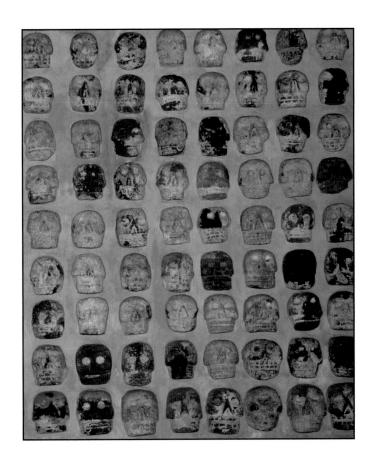

BRIAN FAGAN
General Editor

Tenochtitlan

Leonardo López Luján
and Judy Levin

OXFORD
UNIVERSITY PRESS

Aztec frog sculpture from the Great Temple, 1440–1469.

To Laura, Mariana, and Emilia—L. L. L.
To my Laura—J. L.

OXFORD
UNIVERSITY PRESS

Oxford University Press, Inc., publishes works that further
Oxford University's objective of excellence
in research, scholarship, and education.

Oxford New York
Auckland Cape Town Dar es Salaam Hong Kong Karachi
Kuala Lumpur Madrid Melbourne Mexico City Nairobi
New Delhi Shanghai Taipei Toronto

With offices in
Argentina Austria Brazil Chile Czech Republic France Greece
Guatemala Hungary Italy Japan Poland Portugal Singapore
South Korea Switzerland Thailand Turkey Ukraine Vietnam

Design: Kinglsey Parker   Layout: Alexis Siroc

Library of Congress Cataloging-in-Publication Data

López Luján, Leonardo.
  Tenochtitlán / Leonardo López Luján and Judy Levin.
    p. cm. — (Digging for the past)
  Includes bibliographical references and index.
  ISBN-13: 978-0-19-517851-7
  ISBN-10: 0-19-517851-3
  1. Templo Mayor (Mexico City, Mexico) 2. Indians of Mexico—Mexico—Mexico
City—History. 3. Indians of Mexico—Mexico—Mexico City—Antiquities. 4.
Excavations (Archaeology)—Mexico—Mexico City. 5. Mexico City (Mexico)—
Antiquities. I. Levin, Judy. II. Title. III. Series.
  F1219.1.M5L67 2005
  972'.53—dc22

                                                            2005021703

9 8 7 6 5 4 3 2 1
Printed in Hong Kong on acid-free paper

Picture Credits: Courtesy Proyecto Templo Mayor: 19, 24, 26, 27, drawing by Luis Barba and Agustin
Ortiz: 32, photograph by Salvador Guilliem: 29, 30, 36, photograph by Leonardo López Luján: 5,
33, 45; Picture taken and published by Leopoldo Batres, *Exploraciones arqueologicas en las Calles de las
Escalerillas, ano de 1900, Mexico, Tipografica y Litografia "La Europea"*, 1902: 25; Biblioteca Medicea Laurenziana,
ms. Med. Palat. 219, c. 373r Su concessione del Ministero per i Beni e le Attività Culturali: 15; ©
The Trustees of The British Museum: 3, 4; William Bullock, *A Description of the Unique Exhibition Called
Ancient Mexico*: 23; Codex Magliabechiano: 40; Hernan Cortes, *Cartas de Relacion*, Nuremberg Edition (in
Latin), 1524. Wood Engraving: 11; Fray Bernardino de Sahagun, *Florentine Codex*: 9; Fray Diego Duran,
Historia de la Indias de Nueva Espana e Islas de la Tierra Firme: 13, 16; Courtesy of Leonardo López Luján: cover,
3, 14, 34, 41 (top), 43; Library of Congress, Rare Book and Special Collections: 21; Schalkwijk /
Art Resource, NY: 20; Shutterstock: 46; Werner Forman / Art Resource, NY: 8, 19; Rafael Ximeno y
Planes and Joaquin Fabergat: 17; © Michel Zabé: 1, 37, 38, 44; Richard Zalk: 41 (bottom)

Cover: *Rafael González, Tomás Cruz, and Leonardo López Luján (from left to right) examine a 15th-century Aztec offering.*
Half title page: *Sculptures of human skulls decorate the wall of a building in Tenochtitlan.*
Title page: *Mosaic mask of Quetzalcoatl, 15th–16th century.*
Table of contents: *Turquoise mosaic of a double-headed serpent, 15th–16th century.*

Contents

Where and When

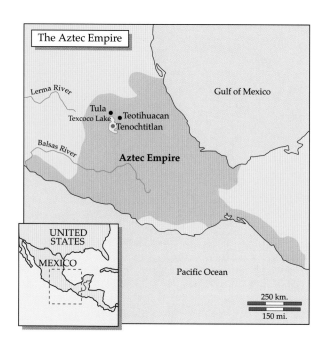

The Aztec Empire

Lerma River
Tula • Teotihuacan
Texcoco Lake • Tenochtitlan
Gulf of Mexico
Aztec Empire
Balsas River

UNITED STATES
MEXICO
Pacific Ocean

250 km.
150 mi.

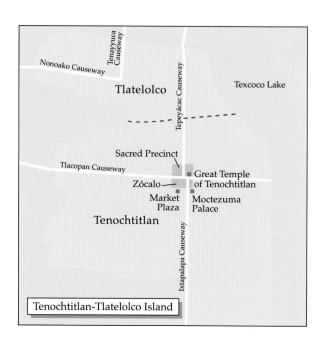

Nonoako Causeway
Tenayyuca Causeway
Tepeyácac Causeway
Tlatelolco
Texcoco Lake

Sacred Precinct
Tlacopan Causeway
Zócalo — Great Temple of Tenochtitlan
Market Plaza — Moctezuma Palace
Tenochtitlan
Ixtapalapa Causeway

Tenochtitlan-Tlatelolco Island

Ancient History

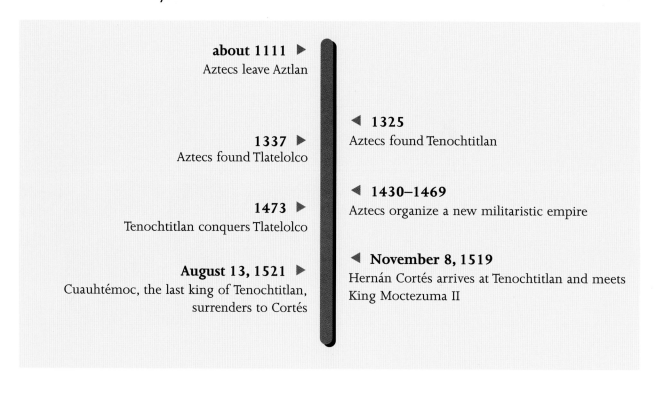

about 1111 ▶
Aztecs leave Aztlan

◀ **1325**
Aztecs found Tenochtitlan

1337 ▶
Aztecs found Tlatelolco

◀ **1430–1469**
Aztecs organize a new militaristic empire

1473 ▶
Tenochtitlan conquers Tlatelolco

◀ **November 8, 1519**
Hernán Cortés arrives at Tenochtitlan and meets King Moctezuma II

August 13, 1521 ▶
Cuauhtémoc, the last king of Tenochtitlan, surrenders to Cortés

Archaeological History

August 13 and December 17, 1790
◄ Workers discover the statue of Coatlicue and Stone of the Sun in Mexico City's main plaza

1792
◄ Antonio de León y Gama publishes his study about these sculptures

1825
◄ National Museum is founded at the National University, in downtown Mexico City

1880
◄ Inauguration of the new museum at the old mint

1900
◄ Leopoldo Batres excavates below Escalerillas Street

1913
◄ Manuel Gamio discovers the southwest corner of the Great Temple

1960
◄ Ignacio Marquina publishes his last hypothetical model of the sacred precinct of Tenochtitlan

1968–1970
◄ Archaeologists discover temples, offerings, and sculptures while constructing the metro, or subway

February 21, 1978
◄ Electrical workers accidentally discover the Coyolxauhqui stone

1978–present
◄ National Institute of Anthropology and History sponsors the Great Temple Project

October 12, 1987
◄ The Great Temple Museum is inaugurated

1

The Fall of Tenochtitlan

A 20th-century artist imagined what the island cities of Tenochtitlan and Tlatelolco may have looked like in the 16th century. The island was less than six miles square and home to more than 200,000 people.

Long before modern archaeologists began to excavate the ruins of the island city of Tenochtitlan—inconveniently located under modern Mexico City—the Aztecs were already digging for the past. In the 1400s, they explored the ruins of Teotihuacan and Tula, which had been destroyed hundreds of years earlier. Awed by the remains of huge pyramids, the Aztecs believed they had found cities built by giants or even by gods. They dug up mounds covered with plants and found buildings containing burials and offerings to the gods: masks, figurines, vessels, and ornaments, all made of stone and ceramic.

The rulers of Tenochtitlan used archaeological discoveries to help establish their power, by linking their civilization to that of prestigious ancestors. When the Aztec people migrated to the Basin of Mexico about 1250 CE, they had no power and no land. They settled in a bleak wasteland where the other peoples of the region hoped they would be killed by snakes. Instead, say Aztec legends, they ate the snakes and thrived. In the early 1300s, the Aztecs' enemies drove them to the shore of Lake Texcoco and then to the swampy islands in the lake. Again they flourished, and in 1325 they founded their island city, Tenochtitlan.

By 1430, they had begun to create one of the largest empires in the Western Hemisphere. They expanded the islands by fencing in part of the shallow lake with wooden stakes and then creating a landfill of clay and stones planted with slender trees. They made war on neighboring cities and towns, forcing them to deliver tribute—taxes paid with goods such as elaborate warrior suits, cotton cloaks, corn, beans, honey, incense, feathers, jade beads, gold, and turquoise. They built a city even bigger and grander than Teotihuacan and Tula had been.

The Aztecs began their "archaeological" activity as they were expanding their empire. They had laid out their city in a grid like Teotihuacan's. Then, in the 1400s, their artists began to imitate the styles of some those older cities' buildings, wall paintings, and sculptures. This was a clever strategy for a people who intended to rule the world. By borrowing from the past, they demonstrated that rather than being the most recently arrived nobodies of the area, they were instead the heirs of these ancient powers. *And* they could beat almost everyone else in battle.

An Aztec man waits for the little breath of smoke that will show him where to dig for precious stones. Aztecs believed that both gems and ancient relics would reveal themselves in this way.

The Sun Pyramid in Teotihuacan, which is more than 215 feet high, gets its name from the fact that the Aztecs thought it was dedicated to the sun god. But archaeologists now think that the Teotihuacanos prayed to the storm god here.

Teotihuacan and Tula had been burned and razed, the first in about 600 CE and the second in 1150 CE. To the Aztecs, this reinforced a fundamental belief that everything has a life cycle, just as animals or plants do. Four times, they believed, the world had been born, had grown, and had been destroyed by the gods. They themselves lived in the fifth and last era. The Aztecs were convinced they could rule the world, but not forever. Something had crushed even the cities of the gods and giants, and it would happen to them.

The destruction of the Aztecs began in 1519.

On November 8, the Spanish conqueror Hernán Cortés and 500 Spanish soldiers stood in a mountain pass above Tenochtitlan and were amazed. As they came down the mountain they saw an island city of more than 200,000 people in a shining blue lake, connected to the mainland by great causeways, wide, flat roads built across the lake. Tall "towers" (as the Spaniards called the pyramids) seemed to rise from the water itself. As they came closer they could see that the city gleamed with white stucco. Canals, like those in Venice, Italy, ran alongside many of the wide, straight streets. Bigger, cleaner, more elegantly laid out than any European city of the time, Tenochtitlan seemed an enchantment, a city from a storybook, so astonishing that some soldiers asked if it was a dream. It was the most beautiful city in the world, Cortés wrote to his king, Charles I of Spain.

No one knows who destroyed Teotihuacan or Tula, but we do know what happened in Tenochtitlan. For more than a week, Cortés and his startled troops inspected the city. As the guests of King Moctezuma II they visited the royal gardens, pools, and houses of birds and beasts from all over the empire, including parrots, eagles, jaguars, pumas, wolves, and snakes. They marveled at the market of Tlatelolco, on the northern half of the island, once a separate city but conquered and absorbed by Tenochtitlan in 1473. There, merchants speaking different languages sold things made of gold and silver, gems, dyes, textiles, clothing, pottery, feathers, flowers, medicines, slaves, and live animals. People could have their hair washed and cut there and eat at refreshment stands. Many thousands of people shopped at the market every day, and a panel of judges watched over it to enforce its rules and punish robbers and cheats.

Aqueducts brought fresh water into the island city from the mainland. Workers cleaned the streets daily and collected garbage. Public toilets allowed human waste to be removed from the city. By contrast, the Spanish city of

In the 16th century, an artist drew this map of the island city of Tenochtitlan-Tlatelolco and several surrounding cities and towns for the Spanish conqueror Hernán Cortés. The sacred precinct, Moctezuma's palace, the zoo, and the royal gardens are in the center.

Seville—with 60,000 people—was the largest many of the soldiers had seen, and the streets of many European cities streamed with filth. Aztecs bathed daily; Europeans thought bathing would make them sick.

But, parts of the Aztecs' culture, especially their religion, horrified the Spanish. Each neighborhood had its own temple-pyramids standing tall among the flat-roofed white houses, but there was also a central sacred precinct, or religious district. It contained many shrines and temples; a school for the nobility; courts for playing a Mesoamerican ballgame that had religious significance; wooden racks where skulls of sacrificial victims were displayed; and the Great Temple. The flat-topped stepped pyramid of the Great Temple—as high as a ten-story building—was crowned by two chapels.

One chapel was dedicated to Tlaloc, god of rain, life, and growth, the other to Huitzilopochtli, the sun god who was also the god of war. Above the entrance to the chapel of Huitzilopochtli was a panel of carved skulls. According to the Aztec creation myths, gods had given their lives to create this world, and humans had to repay that debt. The Aztecs made offerings of blood, including human sacrifices, to ensure that the sun would rise and move across the sky each day and that the earth would give forth enough food. The Great Temple was the center of the Aztecs' world—the place where they gave gifts to the gods to keep alive the fifth era, and the place where they showed their power.

The Spanish soldiers were confused by these people who seemed "civilized" in so many ways but who also cut out people's hearts and offered them to demonic "idols." But the Spanish had not come to the Basin of Mexico precisely to study the Aztecs' religion. They were *conquistadores*—literally, conquerors—who had come to claim the land for Spain and as much gold as possible for their king and themselves. When Moctezuma II, not sure what to make of these oddly colored, oddly dressed strangers, gave presents to Cortés and his men, "[the Spaniards] seized upon the gold as if they were monkeys," an Aztec witness reported later to a missionary friar. "They wanted to stuff themselves with it as if they were pigs." And, the Spanish believed it was their duty to make Christians of all people.

At the foot of the Great Temple pyramid, on the left side of the drawing, is the coatepantli, *a patio surrounded by a wall of serpents. To the right is the* tzompantli, *or skull rack, a wooden structure where the heads of executed prisoners of war were exhibited.*

On August 13, 1521, at dawn, Cuauhtemoc, the last king of Tenochtitlan, surrendered to Cortés. Histories of the conquest often attribute the victory of a small group of Spaniards over an overwhelming number of Aztecs to superior armor, military tactics, and weapons (guns, horses, and attack dogs). Guns and strategy helped, but the Spaniards' real strength lay in Cortés's ability to forge alliances with Moctezuma's enemies and even some of his subjects, for whom paying the tribute that had made Tenochtitlan so beautiful was a burden. Also, many people of the city had died of smallpox, one of the diseases brought by the Spanish that wiped out much of the native population of the New World.

The fighting ended with a four-month-long battle waged in the city streets. Much of the city had been destroyed by then. The

Spaniards and their allies burned the royal bird and animal houses and gardens, turned to rubble many of the palaces and pyramids they had so admired, and used the wreckage to fill in the canals. At first the stink of rotting flesh made the city uninhabitable. But soon, on top of the ruins of Tenochtitlan, the Spaniards began to build Mexico City, the capital of the colony they called New Spain. For the next 250 years the Spanish continued to erase the Aztecs' material culture. They destroyed statues and burned most of the manuscripts. Yet, the Aztecs and the other native peoples of Mesoamerica remained. Their languages, including the Aztec language, Nahuatl, are still spoken. The city and empire was obliterated, but the people were not.

This statue portrays the Aztec fire god as a wrinkled old man, toothless and almost blind. He was one of the most important deities in Mesoamerica, and the Aztecs believed he lived in the exact center of the world.

During the colonial period, the Spanish settled in cities, "civilized" the surviving native peoples by making them Catholic and Spanish-speaking, and employed them. Aztecs worked as farmers and miners. Skilled native stone masons and artists built the Spanish churches and the conquistadors' mansions in Mexico City— carefully hiding carvings of their gods in the columns of the cathedral.

Some of the missionary friars who came to convert the Aztecs to Catholicism were interested in their culture. Like doctors, said the Spanish friar Bernardino de Sahagún, missionaries must understand an illness in order to cure it. To them, the "illness" was the Aztec religion, and Sahagún worked hard to understand those beliefs (and all of Aztec culture) completely. His efforts resulted in a 12-volume encyclopedia of the Aztec world. Having burned and buried the city, the Spanish then hid

The Florentine Codex

The work of the archaeologist is not only to dig up things but to understand them. But how do we understand the objects left by people long gone? We need to identify them, to learn how they were made and to understand what they were used for. What did they mean to people? An archaeologist cannot ask these questions directly of the people they study, but friar Bernardino de Sahagún asked the Aztecs these questions for us.

Sahagún was born in Spain in about 1499. He went to New Spain in 1529 as a missionary and died there at age 90. He learned the Nahuatl language fluently and became convinced that in order to teach people about Christianity he first had to understand their culture. Sahagún submitted a questionnaire to educated nobles and encouraged people to talk about their lives before the conquest.

His work resulted in a 12-book encyclopedia of the Aztec world—the gods, the people, the animals, the plants, the minerals, and the Spanish conquest. He wrote down, in Spanish and Nahuatl, the speeches that noble fathers memorized to recite to their children. (Fathers told boys not to sleep all day and girls not to wear too much makeup or chew gum.) Survivors of Tenochtitlan and people from nearby cities painted pictures into the pages of the encyclopedia. They described and drew Cortés's ships, his warhorses ("deer as tall as roof terraces" they had said at first, having never seen horses), their armor, and their guns (so loud that the noise "shut off one's ears").

Sahagún called his encyclopedia *General History of the Things of New Spain*. Today, it is also known as the Florentine Codex; codex means a book in manuscript, and it is called "Florentine" because it is kept in a library in the Italian city of Florence. Even by modern standards, it is a remarkable piece of scholarship.

This page of the Florentine Codex explains how the Aztecs prepared feathers to be used in such things as headdresses, fans, shields, and capes. The right column explains the process in the Aztec language, Nahuatl.

the work of Sahagún and other friars deep in private libraries and convent archives. People in New Spain and Europe learned the history of the conquest as the Spanish told it. Cortés, the soldier Bernal Díaz del Castillo, and others had written detailed chronicles of the Spanish defeat and the Aztec people. Nevertheless, through the next hundreds of years, as writers borrowed from earlier writers, the story grew muddled. Cortés had described the Great Temple, with its two straight staircases and its two shrines on top. Later historians drew and described the temple with spiral staircases. European historians doubted the truth of the conquistadors' tales about the Aztecs. They argued that "primitive Indians" could not possibly have built a great city by themselves. After all, they had no oxen or other draft animals or wheeled carts. They had no iron tools. They cut people's hearts out for their horrific idols. Perhaps visitors from the lost island of Atlantis had helped them. Perhaps they learned to make pyramids from the Egyptians.

Among modern archaeological sites, Tenochtitlan is unusual.

Six priests perform the most common type of Aztec human sacrifice: heart extraction. Five of them hold the victim while the sixth cuts open his chest with a flint knife. The heart and blood were usually offered to the sun to ensure its daily movement through the sky.

An archaeological site is a mystery to be solved. Usually, archaeologists find the remains of a civilization and ask, "What was this place? Who lived here? What did they believe?" It was the opposite case with Tenochtitlan. Natives and Europeans had written thousands of pages about the city. Archaeologists had the answers to many of these questions but little physical evidence of the city. No one was even certain where the Great Temple had stood.

This all changed in 1790.

2

Rescuing the Past

In this 1810 engraving of the Plaza de Armas, today known as the Zócalo, the Palace of the Viceroy is on the right and the Metropolitan Cathedral is on the left. It was during the restoration of this plaza in 1790 that the Stone of the Sun and the Coatlicue sculpture were discovered.

On August 13, 1790, the same day that Tenochtitlan fell to the Spaniards 269 years before, workers leveling and paving the main plaza of Mexico City found a three-ton, eight-and-one-quarter-foot-tall stone image of the earth goddess Coatlicue wearing a skirt of intertwined rattlesnakes. Four months later and 100 feet away, workers discovered a 24-ton deeply carved stone disk almost 3 feet thick and 11 feet wide. These were startling finds—massive and mysterious evidence of the conquered Aztecs. Buried in colonial rubble, these monuments had obviously been moved from their original sites. Probably the conquerors had found them too big to destroy.

The colonial ruler, the viceroy, Juan Vicente de Güemes y Pacheco, second count of Revillagigedo, ordered the round stone to be displayed at the Metropolitan Cathedral's western tower, and the earth goddess to be brought to the university, where she could be studied. These decisions show how colonial attitudes toward the Aztec past had changed since the conquest. Earlier rulers, beginning with Cortés, had ordered all Aztec monuments destroyed. The Spaniards had dismantled buildings and reused the stones to make the foundations of new ones; they smashed religious sculptures. Conquest required the destruction of the past.

Of course, many artifacts from before the conquest had survived. Cortés had sent objects of gold, silver, precious stones, and feathers back to Charles I. The German artist Albrecht Dürer wrote in 1521, "I have never in my life seen things that so gladdened my heart as these did. Because amongst them I saw astounding works of art and I marveled at the subtle skill of the men of those distant lands." Still, most were destroyed.

During the three centuries of colonial rule, so much looting of graves and archaeological sites went on in Mesoamerica that the Spanish government issued looting licenses. Even native people excavated their ancestors and sold artifacts from the burial sites to pay their taxes. The Catholic friars and archbishops also contributed to the destruction. For instance, one friar, Benito, worked to gain the trust of some Indians until they at last showed him their treasure, a beautifully carved god. The zealous friar then crushed the god to powder to prevent its worship. When archeologists describe this event, a careful reader can almost hear them grinding their teeth in frustration.

But by the middle of the 1700s educated Europeans and *Criollos*—people born in the New World of European parents—were thinking about the past in a new way. Like the Aztecs, who used ancient relics to validate their right to rule, the *Criollos* wanted to use Mesoamerica's pre-Hispanic past for their political purposes. In part, they were reacting to European ideas about the inferiority of the New World cultures. During the 1700s, in a period called the Enlightenment or the Age of Reason, Europeans began to study the differences among groups of people.

Enlightenment thinkers believed that human cultures evolved from "savage" societies, like the Aztecs, to civilized ones, like the Europeans. They looked for "scientific" explanations for the differences among people, and some suggested that the climate in the New World was the reason the Indians were less evolved than the Europeans. (Also for animals: the New World puma was believed inferior to the Old World lion, for instance.)

The Europeans were prejudiced against the New World in part because some Enlightenment thinkers believed that anyone different from them was not as good. Also, they were describing societies that the Europeans had nearly destroyed, so they were not considering the New World cultures at their height. And, finally, most of the Enlightenment writers had never even been to the New World.

Many scholars in New Spain were interested in Enlightenment ideas about liberty and human rights, but they thought these explanations of the New World were both rude and incorrect. And, they were annoyed at Spain for other reasons. The late 18th and early 19th centuries were times of independence movements. Just as the North American colonies grew tired of foreign rule and high taxes and rebelled in 1776, the *Criollos* of New Spain were tired of being taxed and ruled by a faraway government. The *Criollos* used archaeology and history to provide an identity for a new nation, composed of *Criollos*, native peoples, *mestizos* (people who were a mixture

Upon its discovery, the Coatlicue sculpture was put on display at the National University, in Mexico City. But when local people came to worship it, the university authorities, who did not believe in idol worship, had it buried.

of Indian and Spanish), and the minorities of mixed Indian, African, European, and Asian descent.

An astronomer who lived in Mexico City named Antonio de León y Gama made the first serious study of the archaeological finds of 1790. In his book *Descripción Histórica y Cronológica de las dos Piedras* (Historical and Chronological Description of The Two Stones), he wrote that he wanted to show "some of the vast knowledge that the Indians... possessed in arts and sciences." He objected to the description of the Aztecs as irrational or simple, because it belittled Spain's accomplishment in conquering them. Using written sources and codices and his knowledge of the Aztecs' language, Nahuatl, León y Gama analyzed the round stone, which he called the calendar stone.

León y Gama correctly identified the center image as the sun, surrounded by the signs of the four earlier eras that came before the Aztecs' fifth era, and then by the 20 days of the Aztec divinatory calendar, which had 260 days. But he could not understand its function. He erroneously believed the stone was an astronomical marker and a solar clock.

León y Gama had even more trouble explaining the image of the earth goddess, although he was impressed that she had been carved without the use of metal tools. The huge sculpture had giant claws, two serpents instead of a head, and a necklace of human hearts and hands. He incorrectly thought the statue was of Teoyaomiqui, a goddess who collected the souls of warriors in the battlefield, as well as those of sacrificed captives. He believed her head of serpents was a mask and mistook the hearts on her necklace for incense bags.

Carved into the center of the Stone of the Sun is the face of the sun god, and surrounding it are the five mythic eras. Aztecs lived in the fifth and last era and believed gods had destroyed the four preceding eras because humans were imperfect beings.

By 1800, the professors of the university, who were members of the order of monks called Dominicans, had reburied the goddess. They thought the students should see the beautiful white casts of Greek and Roman sculptures that King Charles IV of Spain had sent them,

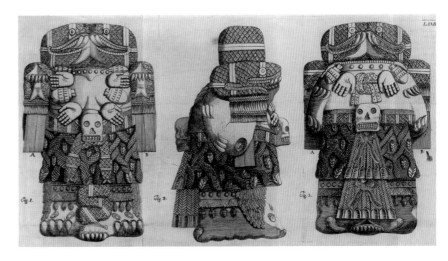

Astronomer Antonio de León y Gama published these drawings of the earth goddess Coatlicue shortly after the sculpture was discovered in 1790. Although her features might seem terrifying to us, to the Aztecs she was a beloved goddess.

not an ugly idol. Possibly they feared that the goddess would revitalize the Indians' traditional religion, which was a realistic concern. In the same way that native peoples of Mesoamerica had learned Spanish but kept their original languages, they adopted Catholicism by mixing its teachings with their older beliefs and rituals. One priest had concluded glumly that the introduction of Christianity meant that instead of having 1,000 gods, the Aztecs had 1,001. In 1805, a bishop wrote that the local Indians could not be prevented from worshiping the stone goddess. As soon as the guard's back was turned, they would kneel before the goddess, burn candles, and leave flowers. The university authorities unburied the stone for Alexander von Humboldt, who undertook a scientific expedition in New Spain between 1803 and 1804, and then reburied it.

When an entrepreneur named William Bullock traveled from England in 1823 to the new Mexican Republic—a war of independence had freed the country from Spain in 1821—to see the statue it was still buried. Having suffered considerable inconvenience to come to Mexico, including a transatlantic boat journey and a stay in a country inn where he awoke to find himself covered in droppings from the chicken roosting above his bed, he was able to make a cast of the statue for his exhibition in London.

Bullock was happily shocked. In 1824 he wrote, "I had the pleasure of seeing the resurrection of this horrible deity, before whom tens of thousands of human victims had been sacrificed, in the religious and sanguinary [bloodthirsty] fervour of its infatuated worshippers." He described her as a "colossal and horrible monster" who was a cross between a deformed human figure and "all that is horrible in the tiger and rattlesnake." Bystanders who gathered to watch the unearthing of the statue expressed contempt for the monolith, wrote Bullock, except the Indians, who were silent and respectful.

Back home in England, in 1824, Bullock exhibited copies of many codices and casts of Coatlicue, the Stone of the Sun, and others, as well as original objects he had acquired or borrowed. It was the first modern exhibition of Mexican archaeological artifacts. Bullock's exhibition introduced 19th-century Europeans to Aztec culture, and it also contributed to the Mexican government's awareness that it needed to preserve its national treasures before foreign collectors illegally removed them. In 1825, the first national museum was opened in Mexico, creating a place where archaeological finds could be exhibited, studied, and preserved.

During the 1800s, Mexico had two emperors, many presidents, and two dictators. The United States invaded in 1846, and France in 1861. Yet, historical and archaeological study continued. Mexico was (and remains) a poor country looking for its own identity. Archaeologists' discoveries about Mexico's pre-Hispanic past—its "roots"—helped create that identity and fuel national pride.

During much of the 1800s, archaeologists and historians made progress by interpreting all types of evidence. As more of the colonial Spanish and native books and codices were published, scholars argued about the exact location of the ceremonial precinct, the ritual enclosure of Tenochtitlan that housed the Great Temple, and tried to understand what this pyramid looked like and what rituals were conducted there.

In 1888, the Mexican historian Alfredo Chavero used written sources to correctly identify the goddess statue as Coatlicue, the earth goddess, source of everything, with the power to make things grow. She is the symbol of fertility, whom the Aztecs sometimes called "our mother." Bernardino de Sahagún had recorded her story in the 1500s, but it was not published until 1829–1830.

Coatlicue was an old woman, says the myth, who lived at Coatepec—Snake Mountain. She had a daughter, Coyolxauhqui, the

At the 1824 Aztec exhibition at William Bullock's museum, the Egyptian Hall in London, visitors could see casts of the Stone of the Sun (center) and of the Coatlicue sculpture (on the right), as well as many other copies and originals Bullock brought back from Mexico.

The Hall of the Monoliths in Mexico's National Museum opened to the public in 1885. On display at the opening was the Stone of the Sun, leaning against the wall on the right.

moon goddess, and 400 sons, the stars. One day, as Coatlicue was sweeping, she gathered up a ball of white feathers and placed it near her belly, under her skirt. She then realized that she was pregnant. Coyolxauhqui told her brothers to kill their mother for this shameful pregnancy, but the unborn child told Coatlicue not to be afraid. Coyolxauhqui led her 400 brothers in battle to slay their mother. As they were about to kill Coatlicue, her son Huitzilopochtli, the sun god, was born: an adult, armed and richly dressed. First he beheaded Coyolxauhqui and threw her down Snake Mountain. She landed at the bottom in pieces. Then, he killed his brothers.

Chavero was the first historian who understood why Coatlicue was not frightening to the Aztecs. In fact, Chavero said, Coatlicue is beautiful. Her droopy breasts look like those of an old woman who has nursed many children. He was able not merely to identify her but to understand her part in Aztec culture.

A few years later, Leopoldo Batres was the first man to undertake an official archaeological dig in Mexico City, recording, drawing, and taking pictures of his finds—although not under the best possible circumstances.

In 1900, workers began digging up Escalerillas Street (now Guatemala Street) behind the Metropolitan Cathedral to build a long sewer pipe of bricks and cement. Leopoldo Batres made it his mission to stay one step ahead of the pickaxes. He was practicing "rescue archaeology," trying to recover archaeological finds before they were stolen or destroyed. The engineers and workmen were not much help. They were not interested in an archaeological site; they wanted to build a sewer. But his friendship with Mexico's dictator, President Porfirio Díaz, who made Batres General Inspector of Archaeological Monuments, did help. Batres complained bitterly. He worked long hours, often by himself, in a 15-foot-deep smelly, muddy pit, afraid he would catch deadly typhoid fever from the sewage.

Batres annoyed other scholars by blocking their research through his friendship with Díaz, but he did a tremendous service to Aztec archaeology. He was the first person to rescue complete buried offerings to the gods and other artifacts. He also recorded their position in relation to streets and buildings. He published a lavish book of his work containing photographs, drawings, and detailed descriptions of his finds. Discovering the Great Temple was Batres's biggest dream, but he believed, incorrectly, that it was behind the cathedral. In fact, the sewer workers dug a trench right through the Great Temple but neither they nor Batres ever knew it.

Batres was determined, but he had no training in archaeology. Manuel Gamio, trained as an archaeologist and an anthropologist at the International School of American Archaeology and Ethnology in Mexico City and at Columbia University in New York City, was the first to use the new archaeological method, called stratigraphy, in Mexico City.

Some of the objects Leopoldo Batres uncovered in his excavation of Escalerillas Street include two statues of the wind god (in the back row) and a Teotihuacan mask (in the center).

The demolition of a building in downtown Mexico City in 1913 allowed archaeologist Manuel Gamio to uncover the southwestern corner of the Great Temple.

The approach, adapted from geology, literally means the recording of layers. In archaeology it means that—unless things have been moved—the deeper you dig, the older things are. Archaeologists also use pieces of broken pottery called shards, which can be put in order from oldest to newest by recognizing changes in their form and decoration, to establish a timeline of the layers at a dig site. This alters how archaeologists work, as they must record exactly where something is found, how deep it is buried, and what is next to it. It also means that even tiny shards of pottery are important, not just things that are beautiful, complete, or valuable.

In 1913, in the middle of the Mexican Revolution, Gamio excavated one block northeast of the cathedral, where a building was being torn down. This chance move, at last, resulted in the discovery of the Great Temple. He uncovered the southwestern corner of the pyramid with a big basalt sculpture of a feathered serpent's head flanking the staircase. The digs revealed that although the Spaniards had entirely destroyed the Great Temple, inside it were earlier and smaller pyramids that the Spanish had never known about. Gamio used old writings and pictures to identify and understand the new finds.

Archaeologists and historians were trying to put a huge puzzle together, even though most of the pieces were still missing—destroyed or lost under city streets. Each excavation was only a tiny window on the past. Ignacio Marquina was a Mexican architect and archaeologist who worked from the 1930s to the 1960s. He analyzed all the old drawings and descriptions of the sacred precinct and its inner buildings, studied and measured everything that had been discovered in Mexico City, and visited or excavated at sites outside the city to create a hypothetical reconstruction of the Great Temple and its precinct. Other Mesoamerican sites were valuable sources of information because Tenochtitlan's religious buildings were not unique. They followed a regional architectural style. Marquina improved upon his first three-dimensional model of the sacred precinct until 1960. Now, every new discovery can be compared and added to his model.

Yet with all the progress that archaeologists had made, important finds were still only made by chance, as a result of public or private works in downtown Mexico City. During the construction of a metro (subway) line between 1966 and 1968, workers discovered, among other finds, an unusually well-preserved temple dedicated to Ehecatl-Quetzalcoatl, the wind god. Even the temple's plaster walls, sculptures, and offerings were intact. Manuscripts describe temples "with no corners" like this one: it is round. Archaeologists left it in place, near the spot where Moctezuma II and Cortés first met each other on November 8, 1519, although its sculptures and offerings are now in the National Museum of Anthropology.

Archaeologist Manuel Gamio (left) sits with colleagues on one of the two feathered serpents' heads flanking the staircase of the Great Temple. Although the Spaniards destroyed one Great Temple, within and beneath it were earlier phases of the same building constructed just like it.

3

Mysteries of the Great Temple

The Coyolxauhqui stone depicts the moon goddess after she had been beheaded by her brother Huitzilopochtli, the sun god. Huitzilopochtli then threw her from the top of Snake Mountain.

The massive excavation of the Great Temple began with yet another accidental discovery. On February 21, 1978, in the middle of the night, electrical workers were digging at the corner of Guatemala and Argentina Streets, six feet below street level, when one of them hit something hard with his shovel. As he cleaned some dirt off it with his glove, he saw a pinkish stone, deeply carved, and he remembered hearing about the discoveries made when the subway was built, back when he was a boy.

For a week, archaeologists from the National Institute of Anthropology and History (INAH) worked to uncover a human face and then the rest of the body sculpted on the surface of a huge stone disk, more than 10 feet across. The carvings showed the moon goddess Coyolxauhqui, the sister of Huitzilopochtli, identified by the bells on her face—her name means "the one with bells on her cheek"—and by her depiction as a beheaded and dismembered goddess. The site was a little more than 800 feet from where the Stone of the Sun and the statue of Coatlicue had been dug up in 1790.

But the discovery of Coyolxauhqui was different from those earlier monoliths in one critical way. Mexican archaeologist Eduardo

Matos Moctezuma concluded that the sculpture was right where the Aztecs had put her; she had not been moved and reburied by the Spanish. The carving was face up, not down, and it was surrounded not by colonial rubble fill, but by offerings and sculptures related to the lunar, or moon, cult. Scholars knew that the Great Temple was a replica of Snake Mountain because the Aztecs Sahagún interviewed had called the pyramid "Coatepec." But nobody expected an enormous Coyolxauhqui sculpture at the base of this pyramid.

This picture was taken in March 1978, at the start of the excavation of the Great Temple. It was there that two months before, workers installing electric cables had discovered the circular stone moon goddess Coyolxauhqui.

Matos Moctezuma, who bears the name of the Aztec king and jokingly claims to be descended from him, had made plans to excavate in the area of the Great Temple years earlier. Some excavation had been possible, but there was still a city in the way. With the discovery of Coyolxauhqui, the INAH gave archaeologists permission to go forward with a long-term dig. At last archaeologists could do a proper excavation and not a rescue operation.

Working in the center of a big city was a nightmare of noise and pollution. The archaeological teams had to make sure that the buildings at the edge of the site did not collapse. They had to work around the city's underground tangle of pipes, electrical lines, and sewers. But being in a modern city had advantages, too. Experts from the INAH, specialized equipment, laboratories, and libraries were nearby. And, students of archaeology, conservation, and history

Several modern buildings were demolished in 1980 in order to excavate the area where the House of Eagles was discovered. The Great Temple is to the left in the picture.

eagerly provided free labor in exchange for the experience of working on a major and spectacular dig.

The archaeological team laid out a grid of two-meter squares with markers that allowed them to record the exact depth and location of each discovery—the stratigraphic method in practice. The site eventually covered almost 139,000 square feet. Although the emphasis was on unearthing the Great Temple, the archaeologists were also looking for other, smaller buildings around it, and for plazas, murals, sculptures, and buried offerings. They were digging into a past only partly understood from written records and earlier excavations, not only to discover lost objects but also to give them life by understanding their meaning.

This search for understanding required the labor of archaeologists, art conservators (to preserve the finds), geologists (to analyze soil and rocks), biologists (to identify plant and animal remains), chemists (to learn the composition of artifacts and murals), and photographers. Carpenters, masons, and blacksmiths also worked on the dig, making boxes to cover the sculptures, and offerings; ladders; corridors and small bridges; warehouses; tables; and so on. In 1980, there were 600 people working on the site.

Archaeologists used the most advanced technology available. The bulldozers and jackhammers needed to demolish buildings and remove asphalt and concrete parking lots gave way not only to pickaxes and shovels but to sophisticated tools that helped show where buried substructures, statues, and offerings might be. Ground-penetrating radar, magnetometers measuring changes in the strength of the magnetic field, and resistivimeters detecting obstacles to electrical emissions were all used to find hidden objects.

Some tasks went very fast. The workers who removed parts of demolished modern buildings labored all day and night. Archaeologists made new discoveries every day: a big sculpture of a feathered serpent head, a small shrine decorated with human skulls made of stone, a mural painting with the image of the maize god, and an offering of sand, coral, seashells, and shark teeth.

Although workers found things quickly, uncovering the context of their discoveries was a very slow process. For example, to excavate buried offerings, archaeologists worked for hours at a time lying down in a kind of wooden swing, suspended inside the pits. With small spoons, tweezers, tiny paint brushes, bone needles, dental tools, and a miniature hose attached to a vacuum cleaner, they removed the dirt from the items in each offering box— wooden scepters, greenstone masks, gods carved in black volcanic rock called basalt, ceramic containers, coral, bones, and pieces of crocodile. After hours of reaching down from a swing, the archaeologists' faces swelled up from the blood rushing to their heads. It was not comfortable, but it was the best way to see an entire offering without stepping on it.

Everything was photographed, drawn, measured, and described, to record not just the items, but their position in relation to one

Reading the Stucco Floors in the House of Eagles

A computer-generated chemical map of the floors in the House of Eagles allows archaeologists to identify the areas where the most activity took place. The darker areas in the different maps indicate where sacrificial blood was spilled, incense was burned, and meals were offered to the gods.

I n the House of Eagles, there are long stone benches decorated with raised carvings that show processions of warriors who merge in a giant grass ball called a *zacatapayolli*. Aztecs inserted into these balls the bloodstained agave thorns and bone awls they used to pierce themselves during the ritual bloodletting. The carvings suggest that Aztecs made ritual blood offerings in these rooms. Modern scientific methods have proved that they did.

In recent years archaeologists have cooperated with chemists to analyze the chemicals found on the floors of places used for rituals. In the House of Eagles, archaeologists guessed that, little by little, the porous stucco floors absorbed everything poured or spilled on them. If this theory was right, then tests would show high concentrations of certain chemicals in front of the most important ritual places.

Archaeologists laid out a 26-by-22-meter grid. Using drills with special bits, a team of archaeologists, chemists, and restorers removed tiny cylinders from each square meter of the stucco floor. The chemists analyzed the samples and revealed concentrations of albumin, fatty acids, carbohydrates, and other substances. Albumin—the main protein in blood—indicates that bloodletting did happen and shows us where in the room men pierced their own tongues, ears, and legs. Fatty acids are found in oils, fats, or resins, including incense and turkey broth. Carbohydrates are substances with high starch and sugar content, such as pulque, a fermented drink made from the agave plant.

Transferred to a computer, the information from analyzing the floor samples allowed archaeologists to map where the Aztecs burned incense, offered food and drink to the gods, and spilled their blood.

another—the pattern and order in which they were buried—and where each offering was placed in relation to other offerings, buildings, and monuments.

Digging alongside the archaeologists were conservators, ready to begin protecting finds the moment they were revealed, sometimes even freeing fragile artifacts on site. Each object required different care. Conservators cleaned ceramic jars with cotton swabs dipped in distilled water mixed with alcohol. Wooden masks recovered from below the water table had to be kept from drying out, while a human skull of a beheaded warrior might need to be brushed with a fungicide to prevent fungus from growing on it. Being buried in a waterlogged soil destroys some things—copper bells for instance—yet preserves such fragile things as incense and seeds. Working with such care, it could take archaeologists and conservators three to eight months to recover a single offering.

Within three months of Coyolxauhqui's discovery in February 1978, archaeologists discovered parts of the stepped side of the temple and then the massive serpent heads surrounding the base of the pyramid itself—the snakes of Snake Mountain! Soon, like Gamio and other archaeologists, they found older temples under the one the Spanish had destroyed.

The Great Temple was very new at the time of its destruction, probably less than 20 years old. But it was built where a temple had stood since the founding of Tenochtitlan. Archaeologists have found evidence that the temple had been added to, enlarged, or entirely rebuilt 12 times, always leaving the older building

This offering in the House of Eagles, excavated by Leonardo López Luján in 1994, was buried between 1440 and 1469. The stone image is of Xiuhtecuhtli, the fire god.

intact as was common in Mesoamerica. The old temple was covered with "fill"—stones and dirt as well as buried offerings to the gods and sculptures—and then the new one was built around and above it, like the layers of an onion or a nest of boxes.

The oldest temple of Tenochtitlan, a structure of wood and earth whose existence is known from written sources, lies under the groundwater of the modern city. It cannot, for now, be excavated safely, because pumping out the water would damage the site itself and all the colonial and modern buildings around it. But the oldest building that could be partly excavated was built around 1390 and

Surrounded by colonial-era and modern buildings, the excavation site of the Great Temple covers 139,000 square feet in the middle of Mexico City. Archaeologists have uncovered the Great Temple as well as 14 smaller religious buildings.

is an almost complete temple. Only the roofs of the two chapels are missing. Archaeologists have been able to unearth the tip of this building, like the tip of an iceberg: the upper steps of the double staircase, the highest portion of the pyramid and the two chapels at the top. The rest of the building is buried with fill and covered by the water table. But why had the Aztec enlarged the temple so often? Archaeologists, working with geologists and historians, have discovered two probable reasons.

Tenochtitlan was built on marshy islands. Even though the architects of the pyramids supported them on wooden stakes and used a lightweight volcanic stone called *tezontle* whenever possible, sometimes the pyramids began to sink. Also, geologists have identified several levels of mud, each one marking a catastrophic flood. And, the region suffered earthquakes. After each of these events, the Aztecs had to raise the base of the pyramid.

The temple was also enlarged (the Aztecs said) when the god Huitzilopochtli needed a bigger and richer house. We might say, instead, that it was enlarged to justify a war and get new subjects to pay tribute. Toward the end of the work on a temple extension, an expedition was organized to conquer an independent city or town and to obtain prisoners, who were sacrificed for the consecration of the enlarged temple. Governors of friendly kingdoms and those hostile to the Aztec Empire were invited to the event. During the festivities, priests extracted the hearts of the prisoners and buried their heads in the corners of the Great Temple. In this way, its enlargments glorified the military expansion. Each temple extension symbolized, celebrated, and sanctified the expansion of the Aztec Empire. The Great Temple increased in size at least 12 times in 130 years because the empire was growing fast.

The skeletons of a young jaguar and a young wolf were buried between 1481 and 1502. Offerings buried with these animals were ceramic models of flutes and drums, seashells, and beads made of jade and serpentine, which symbolize water.

Since 1978, six field seasons, or periods of excavation, have revealed the Great Temple with its 12 expansions and 14 nearby and smaller religious buildings, all part of Tenochtitlan's sacred precinct. So far, archaeologists have found 139 offerings and more than 9,000 objects, including children's skeletons, bones of marine fish, turtle shells, sculptures of the fire god, ceramic jars with the face of the rain god, masks, musical instruments, sacrificial knives made of flint, obsidian arrowheads, and cotton textiles. Some of these discoveries have confirmed descriptions from the 16th century.

One unexpected find in 2000 was a stone box with a seal of lime plaster. Its airtight seal and waterlogged surroundings had kept the box's contents safe from bacteria, oxygen, light, high temperatures, and acid. Inside were the remains of the ritual costume for a priest or an image of the Temple of Tlaloc, the ancient god whose shrine stood next to that of Huitzilopochtli at the top of the pyramid. The costume included a bark-paper headdress, a wooden mask, a cotton sleeveless jacket, a cotton cape, a couple of cotton and paper bracelets, a ritual gourd containing seeds, parts of a jaguar skin, and cactus thorns used for bloodletting in self-sacrifice rituals. Archaeologists had believed that such items were too fragile to have survived and that they would never have a chance to see them except as codices or sculptures.

Some of the most surprising discoveries have been whole buildings. In 1981 archaeologists found the House of Eagles. The inner rooms contained murals, stone benches, ceramic images, and braziers for burning incense, all perfectly preserved. Two life-sized statues of people dressed as eagles guarded the main door.

In 1994, archaeologists excavating the House of Eagles decided to dig several tunnels because the northern half of the house is under a modern street. Working in tunnels is not comfortable. The Aztecs did not believe in a fiery hell, but in an underworld that is cold, dark, smelly, and wet—quite like an excavation tunnel in Mexico City, say archaeologists. The tunnels are also slippery, because of Mexico City's high water table and clay soil. Plastic doors keep the humidity level high in order to protect the artifacts and murals.

Many months of hard labor in these dank tunnels exposed two large rooms, decorated with wall paintings and containing more than 60 feet of benches. Then archaeologists discovered first the face of one huge sculpture and then the claw of another. Although these images were broken into hundreds of pieces, each piece was in place. They had not found, as they expected, more statues of men dressed as eagles. Instead they had found two statues of the scary and bony Mictlantecuhtli, Lord of the World of the Dead, one of the most highly venerated Aztec gods at the time of the Spaniards' arrival in Mesoamerica. The team of archaeologists trembled with happiness and excitement. Extracting and recording the sculptures

In 1981, archaeologists discovered two ceramic sculptures of men dressed as golden eagles. At first, the life-sized figures were identified as eagle warriors, one of the elite warrior groups of the Aztec, but they are now believed to represent the rising sun.

required another five months of work in the tunnel. Then, in the lab, art restorers spent two years assembling the pieces of these huge puzzles.

During the excavation of one of the ceramic statues, archaeologists removed the earth covering it and found a thin layer of a gritty, maroon-colored substance on its head, shoulders, arms, and back, as though a fluid had been poured on it from above. Archaeologists believed it was very old blood. They took several samples of the material, and tests revealed high concentrations of iron and albumin—the main components of blood. Later chemical studies identified human hemoglobin, the cells that carry oxygen in blood, proving that the god of death statue had been bathed with large quantities of blood from sacrificed people, as represented in a scene from a codex.

Other discoveries—less dramatic than blood-drenched statues—such as the carefully ordered offerings to the gods have been equally interesting to archaeologists. Many of these objects are tiny and may seem valueless. What can archaeologists learn from a stone box containing, for instance, jade beads, conch shells, crocodile skulls, eagle skeletons, turquoise disks, and pendants made from a black mineral called jet?

One of the things the offerings show is the size of the empire from which commercial products and tribute were received. Mineral, plant, and animal experts have identified natural materials

This mask of the face of Mictlantecuhtli, the god of death and lord of the underworld, is made of a human skull, with shell and pyrite (a mineral as shiny as a mirror) for eyes, and flint knives for its nose and tongue. The holes in the forehead were probably filled with curly human hair.

from a wide variety of places—the mountains, the temperate zone of the Central Plateau, the tropical forests, the coral reefs, and the coastal waters, some of them very far from Tenochtitlan. Archaeologists have identified who made the artifacts and where they came from. Few were Aztecs. Most of the objects came from the far reaches of the Aztec Empire, and even beyond its borders. Turquoise for mosaics was brought from the region of the modern states of New Mexico and Arizona. Some objects were antiquities even in the time of Tenochtitlan. One mask was already 2,300 years old when the Aztecs buried it.

The arrangement of the items in each container also holds meaning. Although the Spanish described how the Aztecs tossed precious things into the rubble fill of the pyramid, some offerings were put in stone boxes or urns, or deposited in holes dug out beneath floors. In fact, these items were not "tossed." Instead, they were placed carefully in patterns and layers. Their arrangement can tell us how the Aztec people understood the world and what they were trying to say to the gods through their offerings.

Each time the Aztecs enlarged the Great Temple, Tlaloc's shrine (as well as Huitzilpochtli's) was newly dedicated with rituals that imitated the mythical acts of the rain gods. Some offerings to Tlaloc consisted of round blue jars containing green stone beads that represented drops of water and fertility. Each jar was buried on its side next to a bowl, as though pouring water into the bowl. The arrangement represents a myth that says Tlaloc's helpers pour their precious water from the clouds out of jars to make rain.

We return to the Great Temple, or to an offering, with wonder. Like the Spaniards who first saw Tenochtitlan or the painter Albrecht Dürer we look with amazement at what people created so long ago. At the same time we seek understanding by looking below surfaces. Archaeologists literally go below surfaces using shovels, magnetometers, and computers to show how a building was used. They also go below surface meanings to interpret what an offering meant.

During the last years of the Aztec Empire, ceremonies took place to ask for divine favors. In the midst of ritual dances, the reenactment of mythical scenes, and the sacrifice of war prisoners, a priest invoked Huitzilopochtli and Tlaloc with prayers. Carefully, he arranged the offerings of his people to make a request of the gods—for life, for food, for rain, for victory. Then, for more than 500 years, these messages were lost.

Since 1978, members of the Great Temple Project have recovered much of what had been lost. The temples, the sculptures, and the offerings have once again become a form of communication—not between the Aztecs and their gods, but between those people of long ago and people today.

A priest bathes an image of Mictlantecuhtli, the god of death, with human blood. Aztecs believed that he nourished himself on the bodies and hearts of the dead.

Interview with
Leonardo López Luján

Judy Levin Why did you decide to become an archaeologist?

Leonardo López Luján My mother worked as a secretary to Alberto Ruz, the Mexican archaeologist who discovered the tomb of the Mayan King Pakal in 1952. One summer, when my brother was nine and I was eight, we went to work with Ruz to make money. We washed and marked tons and tons of horrible, eroded Mayan ceramic shards. Still, we repeated the experience each summer with different archaeologists.

My father is a historian at the National University of Mexico. He has dedicated his life to the study of Aztec religion, medicine, magic, and education. I remember all those years visiting museums, ruins, and archaeological excavations.

In 1973 and 1974, we lived in Spain, because my father wanted to continue his research in the archives of Seville and Madrid. There, I bought my first book on archaeology and began collecting stamps with archaeological images from all over the world.

In 1979, when I was 15 years old, I visited the site of the Great Temple for the first time because my father was invited by Eduardo Matos Moctezuma, the project's director.

Then, in 1980, during the summer before beginning high school, I had an

Archaeologist Leonardo López Luján (top) poses next to a sculpture of a barrel cactus he discovered in Mexico City in 2005. Author Judy Levin (below) does some digging of her own at the beach.

overdose of soccer, bicycling, and television. This fatal combination drove me to call Matos Moctezuma and to ask him if he needed some help. He just said, "Come tomorrow at 8 AM to the Great Temple. You know how to get there." And this was my beginning in Aztec archaeology. Since then, I've worked with Matos at the Great Temple. I am very proud of it, because I think this was the best way to learn about archaeology—in the day-by-day work, and not in a classroom.

JL Did you always want to work with Aztec sites?

LLL At the very beginning I wanted to become a Mayanist. In fact, I have Ruz's book about the tomb, signed by him: "I hope you will make big discoveries." I read thousands of pages about this civilization, took a course on the Maya writing system, learned the modern Mayan Yucatec language, and dug later in many Maya sites. But destiny is destiny.

JL What is the funniest thing that has ever happened to you in your work?

LLL My first day in the Great Temple excavation, I excavated a pit on the platform. At one o'clock, my boss, Paco Hinojosa, sent me to wash the shards we'd found. When I came back, I continued digging and suddenly found a ceramic container with a long, long neck. I was really happy: I was the luckiest guy in the world. But then I realized that I was uncovering a modern bottle for tequila! Since then, I always bury strange things for the

rookies—for example, modern reproductions of painted Maya vases. You know, many students do not notice that they are excavating Mayan finds in an Aztec site. But they notice when they read on the bottom of these vases the phrase "Reproducción INAH, México, 2003."

JL What was it like for you working on the Great Temple dig?

LLL Those years were really exciting. All the pedestrians watching our work through metal fences and people following it in newspapers and on TV.

José López Portillo, our polemical president at that time, gave us all the support you could imagine. The president came every week to visit us and show the excavation to distinguished visitors: Plácido Domingo, Jacques Cousteau, Jackie Kennedy, Jimmy Carter, Prince Charles, and many others.

JL What is your most important discovery?

LLL In January 1981 I discovered the richest offering in the history of Aztec archaeology, baptized with the non-romantic name of "Chamber 3," and in 1995 the two impressive life-sized ceramic sculptures of the God of Death. But this is not important, because to a large extent it was a question of luck. The most important discoveries, I think, are when we are able to solve an archaeological problem, for example, when it is possible to connect a find with an explanation about its function and meaning in ancient times.

Glossary

artifact An object created by people, as opposed to one found in nature.

basalt A hard black volcanic rock.

brazier Container in which coals are burned for heat or to burn incense.

causeway A raised road across water that, unlike a bridge, is built up from the land below the water.

codex (plural codices) A hand-written book, especially one of ancient texts with pictures.

Coyolxauhqui (co-yoll-SHAUH-kee) The goddess of the moon, sister of Huitzilopochtli.

Criollos The Spanish word for people born in the New World of European-born parents.

excavate The process of expos-ing something to view by dig-ging it up or uncovering it from the dirt or rocks that hide it.

ground water Water that runs below the surface of the earth.

Huitzilopochtli (wee-tsee-loh-POCH-tlee) The Aztec sun god who is also the god of war.

Mesoamerica The Central and North American region that included what is now Mexico, Guatemala, Belize, El Salvador, and Honduras, that included many different societies and languages.

mestizos People of mixed Indian and Spanish backgrounds.

Mictlantecuhtli (meet-tlan-tay-KOO-tlee) The lord of the world of the dead, specifically of the ninth level of the under-world, where people go if they have died of natural causes, such as illness, instead of dying in battle or childbirth.

monolith A single great stone that has been shaped into a sculpture.

Nahuatl (NA-watl) The language spoken by the Aztecs and still spoken by more than a million and a half Mexicans today.

obsidian A black volcanic glass that can be chipped into sharp blades and knives.

offering Natural objects or artifacts ceremonially given to the gods.

shards Pieces of broken pottery.

tribute Payments in objects or money (including cacao beans and cotton cloaks, used by Aztecs as currency) that must be given to a lord or king, often from people who have been conquered.

The Aztecs buried this ceramic vase in the House of Eagles in the 15th century.

Tenochtitlan and Related Sites

THE GREAT TEMPLE MUSEUM

Zócalo Metro Station
Mexico City
http://archaeology.la.asu.edu/tm

The Great Temple archaeological site and museum features 13 Aztec religious buildings, including the Great Temple. These buildings were part of Tenochtitlan's sacred precinct. The site museum's eight halls exhibit all the treasures recovered at the dig. It has the second largest collection of Aztec art in the world.

TLATELOLCO

Tlatelolco Metro Station
Mexico City

Tlatelolco was the twin city of Tenochtitlan. The site includes ruins of its sacred precinct as well as the 16th-century Church of Santiago and the Convent of Santa Cruz.

HILL OF CHAPULTEPEC

Chapultepec or Auditorio Metro Station
Mexico City

Aztec royal images are carved in a boulder found on the sacred Grasshopper Hill. At the foot of this hill were the water sources or springs that nourished the aqueduct conducting fresh water to Tenochtitlan.

THE NATIONAL MUSEUM OF ANTHROPOLOGY (MEXICA HALL)

Chapultepec or Auditorio Metro Station
Mexico City
www.mna.inah.gob.mx

The National Museum of Anthropology exhibits the largest collection of Aztec art in the world.

A circular shrine dedicated to the wind god is located inside the Pino Suárez subway station in Mexico City.

MALINALCO

Toluca Highway, 40 miles southwest of Mexico City
State of Mexico

About a 30-minute walk from the town of Malinalco, there is a group of Aztec monolithic temples, each one sculpted from the hill themselves. There is a small archaeological and ethnographic museum in the town. The town's 16th-century convent has beautiful murals in its cloister.

TEOTIHUACAN
Pachuca Highway, 25 miles northeast of Mexico City
State of Mexico
http://archaeology.la.asu.edu/teo/

The biggest city in Meso-america during the classic period (150–650 CE) where the Aztecs excavated. The pyramids of the sun and the moon are the tallest in the Basin of Mexico. There are also three museums to visit.

TEPOZTLÁN
Cuernavaca Highway, 45 miles south of Mexico City
State of Morelos

There is a small Aztec pyramid on the top of a hill, about an hour from the town. Inside the temple are the remains of stone benches with carvings. There is an impressive view from the hilltop. In the modern town is a museum with an archaeological collection. There is also an archaeological and ethnographic museum inside the town's 16th-century convent.

TEXCOTZINCO
Near Texcoco, 20 miles east of Mexico City
State of Mexico

The Acolhua lived in Texcoco and were allies of the Aztecs. Together with the people of Tlacopan, they formed the Triple Alliance. The Acolhua royal baths and aqueducts are located on the top of a hill at the site.

TULA
Querétaro Highway, 40 miles northwest of Mexico City
State of Hidalgo

An early post-classic capital (950–1150 CE) where the Aztecs excavated. In the Great Plaza, the building called Pyramid B is crowned with enormous columns in the form of butterfly warriors. There is a museum at the entrance to the site. Carved in the Malinche Hill, on a natural boulder, is an Aztec relief of the legendary lord Ce Ácatl Quetzalcóatl.

Tourists can still visit the pyramids in Teotihuacan, Mexico.

Further Reading

Allen, Tony, and Nicolas Saunders. *The Aztec Empire.* New York: Heinemann, 2004.

Baquedano, Elizabeth. *Aztec, Inca and Maya.* New York: Dorling Kindersley, 2005.

Berdan, Frances. *The Aztecs.* 2nd ed. New York: Chelsea House, 1989.

Day, Jane. *Aztec: The World of Moctezuma.* Niwot, Colo.: Roberts Reinhart, 1992.

Fash, William, and Mary E. Lyons. *The Ancient American World.* New York: Oxford University Press, 2005.

Gruzinksi, Serge. *The Aztecs, Rise and Fall of an Empire.* New York: Abrams, 1992.

López Austin, Alfredo, and Leonardo López Luján. *Mexico's Indigenous Past.* Norman: University of Oklahoma Press, 2005.

Matos Moctezuma, Eduardo. "The Great Temple." *National Geographic.* December 1980, pp. 767–75.

Matos Moctezuma, Eduardo. *The Great Temple of the Aztecs: Treasures of Tenochtitlan.* London: Thames and Hudson, 1988.

Matos Moctezuma, Eduardo, and Felipe Solís, eds. *Aztecs.* London: Royal Academy of Arts, 2002.

McDowell, Bart. "The Aztecs." *National Geographic.* December 1980, pp. 704–51.

Sonneborn, Liz. *The Ancient Aztecs.* London: Franklin Watts, 2005.

Steele, Philip. *The Aztec News: The Greatest Newspaper in Civilization.* Cambridge, Mass.: Candlewick, 1997.

This ceramic sculpture represents Mictlantecuhtli, the Aztec god of death. It was found inside the House of Eagles.

Index

Leonardo López Luján is a senior professor and researcher of archaeology at the Great Temple Museum, National Institute of Anthropology and History in Mexico City. He has been excavating the ruins of Tenochtitlan since 1980 and has directed several projects in Mexico City and Teotihuacan. His book *The Offerings of the Templo Mayor of Tenochtitlan* received the University of Colorado's Kayden Humanities Award and was named an Outstanding Academic Book of 1994 by *Choice* magazine.

Judy Levin is a folklorist, librarian, and freelance writer living in New York City. She is the author of *Life at a High Altitude* and a biography of the children's book writer Christopher Paul Curtis.

Brian Fagan is professor of anthropology at the University of California, Santa Barbara. He is internationally known for his books on archaeology, among them *The Adventure of Archaeology, The Rape of the Nile, Archaeologists: Explorers of the Human Past,* and *The Oxford Companion to Archaeology.*

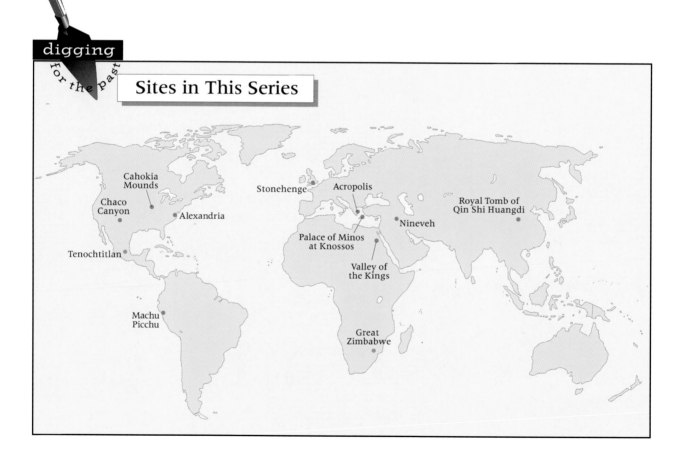

digging
for the past

Sites in This Series

Cahokia Mounds

Chaco Canyon

Alexandria

Stonehenge

Acropolis

Royal Tomb of Qin Shi Huangdi

Nineveh

Palace of Minos at Knossos

Tenochtitlan

Valley of the Kings

Machu Picchu

Great Zimbabwe